Not A
Hollywood Family

Harold Shaw Publishers
Wheaton, Illinois

ANNETTE HEINRICH

To
Dad, Mom, Marc, Dawn, Doug, Adele, Rich, & Brock—
who are certainly not a Hollywood family,
but they're mine!

ISBN #0-87788-584-2
Cover and interior design: K. L. Mulder
Cover photo: Jim Whitmer

Library of Congress Cataloging-in-Publication Data

Heinrich, Annette, 1964-
  Not a Hollywood family.

  Summary: Presents stories and devotions focusing on
communication in the family, relating to siblings, parents,
and other relatives, and handling conflict in family situations.
    1. youth—Prayer—books and devotions—English.
[1. Family life. 2. Prayer books and devotions]
I. Title.
ISBN 0-87788-584-2

98 97 96 95 94 93 92 91 90 89

10 9 8 7 6 5 4 3 2 1

☐ CONTENTS

Week Five: Brothers and Sisters

Week Six: Talk, Talk, Talk!

Week Seven: Family Reunion

Week Eight: All in the Family

Not All It's Cracked Up to Be

☐ DAY ONE

Not a TV Family

Gag me with a TV antenna! thought Greg, as he pointed the remote control at the set and poked "Off." *Sure, life would be just dandy if every family had parents who smiled sweetly at one another all the time, and every family crisis or blowup was resolved with hugs and kisses in thirty minutes, minus commercials!*

They Sure Don't Act Like the Brady Bunch!

That afternoon at Greg's house—one short afternoon—had already seen more family trouble than a whole season of sitcoms.

Coming home from high school, Greg saw a light in the garage and went to check it out. He caught his nine-year-old brother Chris looking at dirty magazines with a friend.

Just as he stuffed the trashy mags in the bottom of the biggest garbage can, Greg's mom stormed out of the house looking for him. His algebra teacher had called to report that Greg's quarter grade was down to D-. He was grounded 'til the end of the quarter.

When Dad got home, he and Mom started with a discussion of Greg's grades, but the fight escalated into some problem with an overdrawn checking account. With all the shouting going on in the kitchen, no one noticed that two-year-old Petey was playing in Dad's open briefcase until Petey had already barfed in it.

Greg had left the silent dinner table early to watch TV.

Fake, Hollywood Families

Fake, Hollywood families usually depict a life of love and harmony that tantalizes the regular, normal family with its perfection. In fact, if Greg keeps comparing his real home life with that model TV family, he's going to go nuts. That life is a fiction—completely unattainable in the real world.

There's another standard for measuring families, and once again Greg's family is going to fall short of it. But so does every family in the whole world. Romans 3:23 says:

> *For all have sinned and fall short of the glory of God.*

You're probably thinking, *Fine! Now I'm really depressed. I'm stuck in an imperfect family with no hope of ever becoming perfect.*

Well, maybe you'll never be the perfect family—in fact, it's pretty unlikely. But you, and maybe your family too, can be transformed by accepting God's great gift of his Son and following God's plan for living in the world. There's more to this passage:

> *For all have sinned and fall short of the glory of God, and are justified freely by his grace through the redemption that came by Christ Jesus. God presented him as a sacrifice of atonement, through faith in his blood.* Romans 3:23-25

God made a way for imperfect people to be saved, a way for imperfect people to come into relationship with him. When God's Son, Jesus, lived on earth, he gave guidelines for how a person should live.

> *The most important one is this: ". . . Love the Lord your God with all your heart and with all your soul and with all your mind and with all your strength." The second is this: "Love your neighbor as yourself."* Mark 12:29-31

God's guidelines for living as a Christian in a tough, imperfect world start with those two most important commandments. If you've never accepted God's great gift of salvation through his Son, do it now. Ask God to help you and your family to live by his guidelines. You won't be a Hollywood family, but you'll be a transformed family, loved and guided by God!

☐ DAY TWO

In Trouble—Again!

"Two weeks!?" Mona's eyes filled with angry tears.

"Two weeks, Ramona. I'm sorry." Mona's mom was firm with the verdict: Mona was grounded for fourteen days—no going out week nights or weekends, and phone privileges limited to a half hour a day.

Mona couldn't argue. She'd broken the house rules for curfew. She stomped down the hall and slammed her bedroom door.

Again!

I'm in hot water again, Mona thought. She wondered if she'd ever learn to stay out of trouble. She had a sixteen-year-old history of scoldings, spankings, groundings, and loss of privileges.

When she was nine, she'd broken six of her mother's crystal glasses in one swift swoop with the telephone cord. She didn't get in trouble for breaking the crystal; she got in trouble for saying that her sister Pamela did it.

"Get a wooden spoon from the kitchen and wait in my room," her mother had said. Then her mom left her in there waiting for almost ten minutes, plenty of time for Mona to think about what she'd done.

After the spanking and the tears, Mona's mom hugged her close and talked with her for a few minutes. "I discipline you because I love you, honey. If I don't help you learn to do what's

5

right, you won't be able to discipline yourself to do what's right someday. I do it because I want you to grow up to be a self-controlled person. I feel terrible because it makes you cry, but I don't know any better way to help you."

Mona felt less furious about being grounded when she remembered what the family's system of discipline was all about.

God's Wooden Spoon

Mona's mom sounds like a pretty smart parent. She's given Mona a good picture of God's purpose in discipline, too.

> *My son, do not make light of the Lord's discipline, and do not lose heart when he rebukes you, because the Lord disciplines those he loves and punishes everyone he accepts as a son.*
> Hebrews 12:5b-6

> *No discipline seems pleasant at the time, but painful. Later on, however, it produces a harvest of righteousness and peace for those who have been trained by it.* Hebrews 12:11

The end result of God's discipline is "a harvest of righteousness and peace." Those who are disciplined by God learn to choose "right." They can rest and relax because they know they are following the Lord!

Sometimes It Hurts

God reminded me through some recent failures that sometimes I'm rather selfish and very impatient. He wouldn't let me forget about those negative aspects of my personality. He waited for me to admit them and ask for his help. Sometimes God's discipline hurts.

Do you sense that the Lord is disciplining you in some area of your personality or your behavior? Write about it here.

_____

_____

Are you willing to take the discipline and let it produce that promised "harvest of righteousness and peace"? Ask God to give you a humble spirit. Thank him for accepting you as his child.

☐ DAY THREE

A Dirty Trick— and How It Turned Out

O nce upon a time, there was a young man who was a mama's boy and a stinker. Until the Lord straightened him out, Jacob was a real creep. Not only did he cheat his twin brother out of his inheritance, but—with a little help from Mom—he stole his brother's blessing, too. Finally Esau got mad enough to kill. So Jacob hot-footed it out of town, and the brothers didn't see each other for a long, long time.

Twenty years later, the Lord told Jacob to move back to his hometown. Jacob had learned to honor and obey the Lord, so he started making plans. One thing bothered him, though. What if Esau still wanted to break Jacob's neck for the rotten things he had done when they were young? So he sent messengers with all kinds of presents to butter up Esau a little before they met face to face.

No Hard Feelings

But those long years of separation had been good ones for Esau, too. He'd become wealthy even without the inheritance he'd lost. He'd learned to honor God. And he'd missed his brother.

So the reunion that Jacob dreaded turned out to be a wonderful day for two brothers. Maybe Jacob and Esau sat down together and talked about the years of friendship they lost because they allowed favoritism, unforgiveness, and a few dirty tricks to come between them. Now that each brother knew where he stood in relationship to God, the problems of their early life became water under the bridge. (Read their story in Genesis 25:23-34; 27:1– 33:20.)

I'll Laugh Later

Don't you just hate it when you're completely depressed or discouraged or heartbroken, and someone (Dad, Grandma, your best friend) says, "You'll laugh about this someday!"? The problems seem so big that you don't think you'll ever feel that good about them.

The people you love the most are the people who hurt you the deepest. But God asks us to trust him to work things out.

> *And we know that in all things God works for the good of those who love him, who have been called according to his purpose.* Romans 8:28

If you have a "wound" from a family battle or a family disappointment, write about it here.

_____

_____

Can you trust the Lord to put forgiveness where there is resentment, and a renewed love where there is bitterness? Ask him to give you the miracle of a joyful spirit in a time of trouble.

> *He [the Lord] has sent me to bind up the brokenhearted,*
> *to proclaim freedom for the captives,*
> *and release from darkness for the prisoners . . .*
> *to comfort all who mourn,*
> *and provide for those who grieve in Zion—*
> *to bestow on them a crown of beauty*
> *instead of ashes,*
> *the oil of gladness*
> *instead of mourning,*
> *and a garment of praise*
> *instead of a spirit of despair.*
> *They will be called oaks of righteousness,*
> *a planting of the LORD*
> *for the display of his splendor.* Isaiah 61:1a, 2b-3

☐ DAY FOUR

I Wish
I Were Adopted

Amy told everybody that she would never, never get married. Her mom and sister laughed at her, sure that she would change her mind someday when she was old enough and Mr. Wonderful came along.

But Amy was absolutely, positively, *definitely* not going to get married. She confessed her reasons only to Beth, her best friend.

Enough Is Enough

"We're a family of failures, Beth," Amy explained. "First, my grandfather left my dad's family when my dad was in high school. That's one marriage down the tubes. Now my parents fight constantly! I just know they'll get divorced, too. There's a pattern of rotten marriages in my family, and I think enough is enough. I don't want to get married just to have someone to fight with all the time or to have kids that I'll drive crazy!"

It's true that Amy's family is caught in a pattern of poor communication, unforgiveness, and lack of commitment. No wonder she feels disgusted with her family. And I agree with her, enough is enough. But I don't think throwing away marriage and the family is the answer. There is a better way to break a pattern of disobedience.

9

Turnabout

Once upon a time there was a king (Solomon) who was considered very wise. And he *was* wise—he built a beautiful temple for God and wrote books to encourage young people to avoid sin and look to the Lord for the meaning of life. But he made one big mistake: he married women who didn't honor God and let them construct temples to their various gods (1 Kings 11:1-4).

The kingdom went downhill from there. King after king came to power in that country, and each one was more evil than the last. They established a pattern of disobedience and hardness of heart.

Then one day an evil king, Amon, died. The Bible says this about him: "He forsook the LORD, the God of his fathers, and did not walk in the way of the LORD" (2 Kings 21:22).

The heir to Amon's throne was an eight-year-old boy named Josiah. Josiah would be the key to breaking the pattern of disobedience to God in that kingdom. The Bible says this about him: "He did what was right in the eyes of the LORD and walked in all the ways of his father [his ancestor] David, not turning aside to the right or to the left" (2 Kings 22:2).

During his reign as king, he discovered a written copy of God's law and determined to obey what it taught.

> *Josiah removed all the detestable idols from all the territory belonging to the Israelites, and he had all who were present in Israel serve the LORD their God. As long as he lived, they did not fail to follow the LORD, the God of their fathers.*
> 2 Chronicles 34:33

You can read the story of Josiah, the king who broke away from the destructive pattern of disobedience, in 2 Kings 22-23 and 2 Chronicles 34-35.

Just One

God used just one young man to make big changes for himself and for his people. God can work that kind of miracle, because he is a God who transforms.

> *Nothing is impossible with God.* Luke 1:37

I can do everything through him who gives me strength.
Philippians 4:13

Therefore, if anyone is in Christ, he is a new creation; the old has gone, the new has come! 2 Corinthians 5:17

You can be different in your family—not in your own strength, but in God's power to change lives. Write down at least three things you would like to *be* different or three things you would like to *do* differently in your family.

_____

_____

_____

Talk to the Lord about each of these things, asking him to change you and to give you courage to stand for what's right in tough situations.

☐ DAY FIVE

Take Me Out to the Ballgame

Phil stared at the computer screen on the desk in his best friend Randy's room, pretending to be absorbed in the Laser Tag program they were playing. Randy's dad had just come home from the city, briefcase in hand and a tired smile on his face.

"Randy, my man!" he said, laying his hand on Randy's shoulder. "Good day today?"

"Yeah, Dad—no major hassles. Mom's out back. Phil is staying for dinner." Randy turned from the game to look up at his father.

"Great. I'll go get cleaned up."

Phil's heart felt icy, but he tried to look like everything was okay. He didn't want Randy to know how much he envied him, how much he missed his own dad.

Phil's parents divorced when he was eleven, and at the time Phil was glad to stop the fighting. He saw his dad often—on Sundays, and for a vacation in the summer. He loved both of his parents and didn't want either of them to be unhappy.

But sometimes Phil felt ashamed of his family. To him his family seemed like a failure. He missed the Saturday mornings when Dad would crawl out of bed early to watch cartoons with him before Mom got up. And he missed the days when Dad would come through the door with tickets in his pocket for a baseball or soccer game. Now, life at his house just wasn't all that family life is supposed to be.

What Do You Think?

Phil isn't the only one who ever felt disappointed with his family—almost everyone wishes once in a while that things were different at home. And Phil is certainly not the only young person who lives at home with one parent.

But knowing he's not the only one to feel disappointed about broken relationships in the family won't help him feel any better. If you were one of Phil's good friends, what encouragement would you give him? Write your encouragement here:

_____

_____

_____

The Sure Thing

At some time in their lives, everybody experiences a broken relationship. Maybe parents divorce. Maybe a best friend moves away and seems to forget all about the friendship. Maybe a boyfriend or girlfriend moves on to someone else. There is only one "sure thing" friendship: a relationship with God.

> *There are friends who pretend to be friends,*
> *but there is a friend who sticks closer than a brother.*
> Proverbs 18:24b

> *. . . I will be with you; I will never leave you nor forsake you.*
> Joshua 1:5

Has another person ever failed you in a relationship?

_____

_____

Have you ever "failed" in a relationship with a friend or family member? Tell about it.

_____

_____

If you are not already part of God's family, ask the Lord today to forgive your sins and to be Lord of your life. You'll be adopted into his forever family.

Thank the Lord right now that he is not like our human friends or family members (or like ourselves!). Thank him that he is a friend who sticks closer than a brother.

And I Have to Live Here!

☐ **DAY ONE**

Two-Faced Sneaks

My father was a two-faced sneak. Three short hours after a shouting match with my brother in our backyard, he talked about ministry and God's will in front of a crowd of people. Hypocrite! Someone should ask me—I would tell them the truth about the man they thought was so distinguished.

Ever had a feeling like this one? Mine was over the minute I stopped being angry and started looking at the facts. The truth was that my dad was cranky because he had too much work to do, and his body hurt from arthritis. And the truth was that he loves my brother a lot, and my brother knows it. And the truth was that my dad loves God and tries to serve him in his work, in his ministry, and in our family.

In the heat of the moment, I wasn't being fair. In the heat of the moment, it didn't seem possible for someone who could be such a big pain to be really great at the same time.

They're Only Human

When you're a kid, your parents are just Mom and Dad. So it's amazing to discover that they are human—people with good and bad days, good and bad personality qualities.

My dad is a great guy. I think he's "a man after God's heart" like David, the king of Israel (1 Sam. 13:14). David was an exceptional king and a national hero, and most of the time you hear only good things about him. But there was a time when he fell, and he fell hard. You can read the story in 2 Samuel 11. Not only did he sleep with another man's wife, he had her husband killed to cover up his sin.

How could a guy with a heart after God commit adultery and murder? That's the way we are—we have an incredible inclination to sin. Thank goodness God is patient and loving and can make the miracle of a clean heart, even after we've disappointed him.

Psalm 51 is David's prayer of repentance to God:

> *Have mercy on me, O God,*
> *according to your unfailing love;*
> *according to your great compassion*
> *blot out my transgressions.*
> *Wash away all my iniquity*
> *and cleanse me from my sin.*
> *For I know my transgressions,*
> *and my sin is always before me. . . .*
> *Cleanse me with hyssop and I will be clean;*
> *wash me, and I will be whiter than snow.*
> *Let me hear joy and gladness;*
> *let the bones you have crushed rejoice.*
> *Hide your face from my sins*
> *and blot out all my iniquity.*
> *Create in me a pure heart, O God,*
> *and renew a steadfast spirit within me.*
> *Do not cast me from your presence*
> *or take your Holy Spirit from me.*
> *Restore to me the joy of your salvation*
> *and grant me a willing spirit,*
> *to sustain me.* Psalm 51:1-3, 7-12

Think of a time when you felt angry with someone who seemed "two-faced" because they failed you. Ask God to help you remember that he loves them and can create a new heart in them.

Think of a time when you were all too human, a time when you did something you felt ashamed of. Use David's prayer to ask God for a renewed heart and spirit.

☐ DAY TWO

God's
Hands

N athan doodled on the corner of his notebook. He was spending his Saturday hanging out in the public library— what a drag.

When he'd crawled out of bed that morning, the first thing he laid eyes on was his brand new stepbrother in the next bed. The second thing he noticed was the room full of model airplanes and Ranger Rick nature posters.

Some room for a seventeen-year-old, he groaned inwardly.

Nathan's mom had remarried exactly a month before, and they'd left their apartment to move in with Nathan's stepdad and his family.

Insta-family, Nathan thought. Except he just couldn't make himself remember that those two little kids were supposed to be "brother" and "sister."

Not an Exact Fit—Yet

Nathan had discovered that little kids take up a lot of time and energy. He hardly talked to his mom anymore except when she needed him to drive the kids somewhere or run an errand.

And she had a husband now, too. Nathan was glad about that, though. He liked his stepfather. But he couldn't help feeling like an extra. So he'd gotten quieter and quieter around the house until he started disappearing—to the arcade at the mall, to his friends' houses, or to the library.

Belonging

Transition times are stressful. It's no wonder Nathan is feeling unconnected and out there all alone.

What situations make you feel "outside" or "alone?" Write about them here:

_____

_____

It might comfort Nathan to remember that God's commitment and attention never change. He's always with you, ready to comfort. There is nothing that can take his love away.

> *I am convinced that neither death nor life, neither angels nor demons, neither the present nor the future, nor any powers, neither height nor depth, nor anything else in all creation, will be able to separate us from the love of God that is in Christ Jesus our Lord.* Romans 8:38-39

> *"See, I [God] have engraved you on the palms of my hands."* Isaiah 49:16

In His Hand

My mom used to have a little statue of a hand with a person carved into it. I loved to remember the meaning of that figurine every time I saw it.

God made the whole universe, and he holds all creation together in his powerful hands. But not only does God make room for you in his hand, he *carves* you there and makes you a permanent fixture in that safe place.

Think about your spot in God's hand. Imagine his love and protection all around you. Then thank him for his amazing, wonderful care.

☐ DAY THREE

Call Him Father

E lena pulled the heavy blue comforter up close to her face and snuggled deep into the unfamiliar bed. *This is it*, she thought, *my new home*.

It was Elena's first night as an official foster child in an official foster family. The Petersons seemed like great people. In one short day, their house had already begun to feel like home.

She's Come a Long Way

It was more than a year ago that Elena had finally managed to tell her mom about the years of abuse she had suffered from her dad. She'd been afraid to talk about it, knowing her mother would be hurt and upset.

She certainly hadn't counted on her mom's fit of rage. Her mother slapped her, called her a liar, refused even to consider the possibility, and finally kicked Elena out of the house completely.

Elena spent some time with an aunt—until her aunt discovered the real reason Elena couldn't live at home. Her aunt reacted almost the same way Elena's mom had, and soon Elena was stranded without a home again.

Samantha, a single lady from her church, took her in for five months. She bought Elena clothes, made her lunches, gave her spending money, and provided a place of love and comfort during those months of court battles and meetings with lawyers.

Ward of the Lord

Now Elena was officially a ward of the state. But Samantha had encouraged her to consider herself a "ward of the Lord."

That morning when Elena had packed up all her things and was waiting for the Petersons to pick her up, Samantha gave her a three-by-five card with these verses:

> *A father to the fatherless . . . God sets the lonely in families.*
> Psalm 68:5-6

> *Be strong and courageous. Do not be terrified; do not be discouraged, for the LORD your God will be with you wherever you go.* Joshua 1:9

> *"I will not leave you as orphans; I will come to you. Before long, the world will not see me anymore, but you will see me. Because I live, you also will live."* John 14:18-19

You, Too

Whether or not you live at home with your own parents, you are God's "ward" if you've given your life to him. Think of a circumstance, past or present, when you really had to be courageous in trusting God. Write about it here.

_____

_____

_____

Spend five whole minutes praising God for being a faithful Father. You might want to make a list of the characteristics that make God a great father (always loving, limitless forgiveness, etc.). Or, use the Psalms to help you praise him.

> *How great is the love the Father has lavished on us, that we should be called children of God!* 1 John 3:1

☐ DAY FOUR

Weight of the World

A t first Ricky spent a lot of time hiding. When his dad came home at night, he'd usually had too much to drink, and Ricky learned quickly that the best way to keep away from the angry words and flying fists was to be invisible.

So Ricky studied at the library instead of at the kitchen table or in the family room. And Ricky got a job after school—a job that kept him away from the house until after the normal supper hour. And pretty soon, Ricky started spending as much time as he could at the home of his girlfriend, Maria. Maria's house was a lot quieter than his own.

#2 Dad

But Ricky couldn't stay away twenty-four hours a day. He had to eat; he had to sleep. He had to check on his brothers. Ricky knew his younger brothers were scared and needed him to be there for them.

When their dad came home, Ricky and his brothers would stay in their rooms, hardly breathing so that Dad wouldn't notice that they were there. But sooner or later, Dad's pent-up anger would discover them. Ricky, being the oldest, caught the worst of the bad language and the slapping hands. But Ricky was glad to take it—he'd rather his dad hit him than his mom or his brothers.

And Ricky's mom had started to depend on him to help

hold the family together. He ran errands for her, drove the younger boys to Little League, talked with her about finances, hugged her when she cried, and listened when she needed to talk.

When their real dad became an un-father because of his drinking, Ricky became Dad #2, taking the weight of the world onto his shoulders.

Help Is on the Way

But Ricky isn't an adult, and he has all the regular responsibilities of school and home. How is he going to carry the family's burdens? Ricky is a Christian, so he goes directly to the power source. God has provided help for Ricky. Jesus is the great comforter and burden-carrier.

> *The LORD is close to the brokenhearted and saves those who are crushed in spirit.* Psalm 34:18

> *Come to me, all you who are weary and burdened, and I will give you rest. Take my yoke upon you and learn from me, for I am gentle and humble in heart, and you will find rest for your souls. For my yoke is easy and my burden is light.* Matthew 11:28-30

At Your House

Maybe the problems in your family are less extreme than Ricky's. Maybe they're worse. But either way, God is bigger than problems of any size, and his offer of help applies to your burden-carrying, too.

Write down two major problem areas you see in your family.

_____

_____

Have you ever talked with God about these problems? Have you asked him directly to take your load of worries and help you?

Only Christians have a God so tender that he is "gentle and humble in heart." Only our God promises "rest for your soul." Praise him for his character of love and gentleness. Ask him for the peace he promises.

☐ DAY FIVE

The Other Brother

E mily felt like kicking the dog. After receiving a great report card, she couldn't wait to show Mom. So she went
directly home from school instead of hanging out with the
other girls. And what kind of response did she get?

"Oh, honey—that's great. Straight *A's*, as usual. But Emily,
don't put it up on the refrigerator. It'll make Ronnie feel bad."

Emily's fourth-grade brother, Ronnie, struggled to make
good grades. He could hardly sit still in class, and Emily's parents
were forever hearing from the elementary school principal. But his
report card hung on the fridge in proud display: an *A*, 3 *B's*, and
2 *C's*.

*What do I have to do to get some attention around here—flunk
out?* Emily fumed.

No Claim to Fame

There's a story like Emily's in the Bible—the story of the prodigal
son. You know the story of the boy who didn't appreciate what he
had, who took his half of the family estate and set out footloose
and fancy free to party with his friends. But when his money ran
out, so did his friends, and the boy ended up going home to Dad,
who welcomed him back with open arms and a party.

But what does that have to do with Emily? The parable be-
gins with these words, "There was a man who had two sons." The
other brother in this story doesn't get much attention. We get so

excited about the picture of God's love and forgiveness in the first part of the story that we neglect the older brother.

No Fair!

The older brother was a good boy. He stayed home, worked his dad's fields, and generally kept out of trouble. Then the black sheep of the family turned up at the house, tattered, hungry, and without a penny, and Dad gave him the best of everything—a beautiful robe, the most expensive food, new shoes, and a huge party. No wonder the older brother hollered, "No fair!"

> *The older brother became angry and refused to go in. So his father went out and pleaded with him. But he answered his father, "Look! All these years I've been slaving for you and never disobeyed your orders. Yet you never gave me even a young goat so I could celebrate with my friends. But when this son of yours who has squandered your property with prostitutes comes home, you kill the fattened calf for him!"*
>
> *"My son," the father said, "you are always with me, and everything I have is yours. But we had to celebrate and be glad, because this brother of yours was dead and is alive again; he was lost and is found."* Luke 15:28-31

Two Prodigal Sons

Both brothers were prodigal sons. That older boy lived in his father's house, "served" in his fields, and had all the father's resources (food, clothes, money) close at hand. But he called his service "slavery" and complained that his father hadn't given him enough.

God wants us to serve him out of love for him—service that comes naturally from having a good relationship with the Father. God wants us to take advantage of the resources of peace, comfort, physical provisions, and joy that he says belong to us, that are ours for the asking. The older son's problem was serious—he lived with his father but didn't understand his father's heart.

It's easy to forget what Christian living is all about. We focus on the work to be done and the do's and don'ts. We completely forget that it's really about living with the Father and understanding his love.

Take time to talk to God about how you've been living for him. Ask him to help you make loving him and understanding his love your top priorities.

Parent
Problems

☐ DAY ONE

Sometimes Mother Knows Best

When I was about fourteen, my mom and I had a disagreement about whether I should be allowed to go to a certain movie with some friends. It wasn't a shouting match, but a good conversation about what we both thought was important. Mom wanted me to respect God's standard of holiness and to stay away from off-color talk and subject matter. I wanted Mom to respect my right to make choices for myself.

In the end Mom said I could decide for myself, and I went with my friends to the movies (of course). But it was like going to the movies with my mom (or Jesus) sitting next to me in the theater. I cringed at every dirty joke and swear word. I was more sensitive than ever to God's standard of purity and realized that the movie was going to stick in my mind a long, long time.

A Wise Mom

My mom had already learned to obey Paul's instructions in Philippians 4:8, and she wanted me to learn, too.

> *Finally, brothers, whatever is true, whatever is noble, whatever is right, whatever is pure, whatever is lovely, whatever is admirable—if anything is excellent or praiseworthy—think about such things. Whatever you have*

29

learned or received or heard from me, or seen in me—put it into practice. And the God of peace will be with you.

I certainly had a lousy time at the movies that day, but I think Mom and I both got what we wanted!

Of course your parents can't be right *every* time—they're only human. But they have lived longer than you, and maybe they've learned something that can save you from trouble (or from a lousy day at the movies!) later on. Give your parents a chance to influence your choices. You may find out that they'll respect those choices you make!

Ask God to help you learn from your parents and to help you be holy. He can give you a teachable spirit, and he promises to give you wisdom if you will only ask. Write out your prayer here. (Look up Psalm 119:33-40 for some ideas!)

_____

_____

_____

_____

_____

☐ DAY TWO

Embarrassing Moms

James and John had an embarrassing mother. Sometimes embarrassing moms are the most loving moms of all, but they give their sons all kinds of trouble. I'll bet you recognize the characteristics of this kind of mom. She's the kind who kisses her kid right on the lips in front of everyone when she drops him off for school. She's the kind of mom who wants to know exactly who her son's friends are and if they're treating him O.K. She's the kind of mom who wishes her son were still small enough to climb up on her lap for heart-to-heart talks.

Is your mom sometimes an "embarrassing mom"? Think of the last time your mom embarrassed you just by being "Mom." Write about it here:

_____

_____

Aw, Mom!

Mrs. Zebedee (the mother of James and John) had her boys' best interests at heart when she went to Jesus and asked if—someday, when he was rich and famous—her boys might become Jesus' right-hand-man and left-hand-man. Now, I don't think James and

31

John really objected to her speaking on their behalf; they were probably used to it.

> *Then the mother of Zebedee's sons came to Jesus with her sons and, kneeling down, asked a favor of him.*
>
> *"Grant that one of these sons of mine may sit at your right and the other at your left in your kingdom."*
>
> *"You don't know what you are asking," Jesus said to them. "Can you drink the cup I am going to drink?"*
>
> *"We can," they answered.*
>
> *Jesus said to them, "You will indeed drink from my cup, but to sit at my right or left is not for me to grant. These places belong to those for whom they have been prepared by my Father."*
>
> *". . . whoever wants to become great among you must be your servant, and whoever wants to be first must be your slave—just as the Son of Man did not come to be served, but to serve, and to give his life as a ransom for many."*
> Matthew 20:20-23, 26-28

Jesus was disappointed that such a question would ever be asked. It demonstrated his disciples' misunderstanding of his kingdom in two ways.

First, many of the disciples didn't understand yet that Jesus was not going to have an earthly kingdom, like that of the Romans who ruled them. He wasn't going to have a throne here at all, but would suffer terribly. His death and suffering were the "cup" that he talked about. He promised the brothers that they *would* share that cup, although they probably didn't know what he was talking about. Eventually they did suffer persecution and death because of their stand for Christ.

Second, Jesus' kingdom has a reverse mentality that these brothers hadn't yet learned—the not-to-be-served-but-to-serve mentality. The Son of Man (that's Jesus) is the example: the one whom God regards as first is the one who serves.

I believe that Mrs. Zebedee and her sons got past the embarrassing-mother stage to understand the service mentality of the Kingdom of God. The Sons of Thunder (James and John) became heroes of the faith.

Jesus is probably often disappointed when our mentality doesn't quite fit the servant system that he intended, but he can turn us into Sons of Thunder if we give our lives over to him in "kingdom living." Ask God to help you serve like his Son, Jesus.

☐ DAY THREE

Sweating It Out

S andy opened one eye and peeked out of the covers at the clock. 6:50—she had ten minutes before Mom would come to make her get up. The light sneaking around the corners of her windowshade and the warmth of Sandy's room told her that it was going to be a hot day. She rolled over and glared at her closet. The door was open, and some of her clothes (the rest were on the floor of the closet or in the hamper) were hanging there. *Ugh. The agony of dressing for school!*

Sandy had an old-fashioned mom—a mom who didn't think girls should wear shorts to school *ever*. Sandy had argued over and over again that all the girls did, that it wasn't against the rules, and she would wear the longest ones she had—almost to her knees! But Mom never budged. And day after day, Sandy sweltered while her classmates could tan their legs at lunch time. Sandy thought about having it out with her mom again this morning. *I don't know which is worse, fighting with Mom or sweating at school.*

What Do You Think?

If Sandy were a friend of yours, what advice would you give her about dealing with her mom? Think through your answer carefully. Try to imagine how your solution would work in your own home.

33

_____

_____

_____

Almost every young person disagrees with his or her parents some of the time. Can you think of a similar area of disagreement at your house? Write it here.

_____

_____

Like it or not, your parents are the ones God gave you, and he had a purpose in choosing them for you. Obeying your parents even when it doesn't seem fair or logical not only keeps the peace at your house, it is obedient to God's Word.

> _Honor your father and mother, as the LORD your God has commanded you, so that you may live long and that it may go well with you in the land the LORD your God is giving you._ Deuteronomy 5:16

> _Children, obey your parents in the Lord, for this is right. "Honor your father and mother"—which is the first commandment with a promise—"that it may go well with you and that you may enjoy long life on the earth."_ Ephesians 6:1-3

There's another good reason to obey your parents, and it's a reason we don't often think about: Obeying your parents is good training for obeying the Lord. There are going to be times in your life when doing things God's way seems unreasonable or even unfair, but God wants you to honor him with your obedience and wait to see what good things he will do with your choices.

Ask God right now to help you talk with your parents respectfully about things that seem unreasonable. Ask him to give you the courage to obey cheerfully even when things don't work out the way you'd like them to.

☐ DAY FOUR

Two-Way Street

Peter: Dad, where'd you put the car keys when you came in? I need to get going.

Dad: Where do you think you're going? I need the car tonight.

Peter: But, Dad! I asked you last week. I checked it out with Mom, too.

Dad: I have a meeting tonight, Peter. I don't want to argue about this.

Peter: That's not fair—I *asked*. I obeyed the house rules for the car. I shouldn't have to give up my rights because your schedule changed . . .

Dad: That's enough, Peter. Don't talk to me that way.

How does this father-to-son exchange make you feel?

_____

In your opinion, who was in the right?

_____

Do you think Peter handled the injustice well?

_____

Has your mom or dad ever been unreasonable like Peter's dad, acting without consideration for your time, your interests, and your plans? These things are bound to happen now and then— even parents who are usually understanding and compromising sometimes have an off day.

It Works Both Ways

It's okay for you to be disappointed when your parents break the rules for "fair" at your house. It's okay for you to expect them to work as hard at your relationship as you have to. God expects them to work at it, too.

> *Children, obey your parents in everything, for this pleases the Lord.*
>   *Fathers, do not embitter your children, or they will become discouraged.* Colossians 3:20-21

God's plan for the parent/child relationship is a logical one. It isn't hard for a child to obey a parent who is trying hard not to embitter or discourage, and it isn't hard for a parent to be considerate and encouraging to an obedient child. Wouldn't life at home be great if everyone in the family took these verses to heart? It's easy to say, but much harder to do.

In in your heart choose to obey God's command in Colossians to obey your parents, and ask God now to help you honor your parents with obedience.

Pick a time when your parents can sit down with you and talk about obedience and consideration, using these verses. Don't wait until a disagreement comes up to talk about it; you may feel angry or upset then. If it's hard to talk about things like this in your family, write your parents a note telling them that you're committed to holding up your end of God's plan.

☐ DAY FIVE

"When I Was a Child . . ."

When Roger asked his dad for a ride to school, his dad said, "When I was a child I walked four miles in blizzard conditions to get to my school . . ." (but he drove Roger anyway). When Roger asked for spending money, his dad said, "When I was a boy I worked two after-school jobs—my folks couldn't give me all the luxuries you've got" (but he gave him the cash). And when Roger begged to move his curfew to 12:30, his dad said, "When I was your age, I got a girl home by 10:00 or I'd have her father to reckon with . . ." (but he let Roger stay out later).

Superteen

Wouldn't Roger be surprised to find out that his father hadn't really been Superteen—that he had once been suspended from school for cutting classes, and that Roger's grandparents had been at their wits' ends with him because he fought with his sister constantly?

Roger's dad wants Roger to develop responsibility, diligence, and consideration. So he conveniently forgets to tell Roger about the "wild times" and concentrates on what he did right.

The Big Picture

Do your parents ever talk about when they were your age—about the struggles and problems, achievements and good times? Write down all the information you can remember hearing about your parents' high school years.

_____

_____

If you've discovered that you really don't have the big picture—the good stuff and the bad stuff—of your parents' teen years, bring up some of these questions at the dinner table:

What grades did you get in Algebra?

Were your parents ever absolutely furious with you?

Where did you go on your first date?

What did you think about church and the Bible back then?

Parents Are People, Too

I was in fifth grade the first time I saw my mother crying—really crying. My dad was out of town, and Mom was left with all of us kids. I came down one day, and she was sitting at the breakfast table with a giant teardrop about to drop off the end of her nose.

It shook me up. When you're a kid you don't think about your parents' feelings. They provide everything you need, and they look after you when you break an arm falling out of a tree or when the bully up the block is after you. They're superhuman.

But once you hit high school, you develop a different relationship with your parents. You learn about their struggles and failures and emotions. You start being a friend to them. Show them you're ready for that adult interaction, and maybe your folks will share their personal lives with you, too. Communication leads to unity.

> *Make my joy complete by being like-minded, having the same love, being one in spirit and purpose. Do nothing out of selfish ambition or vain conceit, but in humility consider others better than yourselves. Each of you should look not only to your own interests, but also to the interests of others.* Philippians 2:2-4

Ask God to give you an open mind about your parents, to help you put aside your own interests to investigate theirs. Ask God to bring his kind of unity to your family relationships: "like-minded, having the same love, being one in spirit and purpose."

Superglue

☐ DAY ONE

Coolest of the Cool

R andy Jones was the coolest of the cool: star basketball player, good student, nice-looking, and popular. He won the election for Student Council president with a landslide vote, became triumphant captain of the speech and debate team, and was crowned Homecoming King—all in his senior year!

"Most likely to succeed . . ." said the teachers at Harper High.

"I'd give anything to be like Randy . . ." said all the students.

After All

When Randy comes home from school he's irritable with his mother if she doesn't have his supper ready. *After all*, he's busy handling all the responsibilities of his success and popularity.

Randy pesters his dad for money constantly, even though he knows the family finances are tight and his parents often go without the things they need. *After all*, a guy with Randy's reputation has got to have spending money to dress cool and hang out at all the right places.

Sandra Jones, Randy's little sister, is a sophomore at Harper High. She'd make his bed and take out the garbage for him for a month just for one moment of recognition or encouragement from her brother. But he breezes right past her in the hallways. *After all*, she's a lowly sophomore, and Randy can't compromise his superior senior friendships by hanging out with her.

All for Nothing

Randy's life seems just about perfect, doesn't it? There's only one problem with all the good things Randy does: God has a different measuring stick from Randy's.

> *If I speak in the tongues of men and of angels, but have not love, I am only a resounding gong or a clanging cymbal. If I have the gift of prophecy and can fathom all mysteries and all knowledge, and if I have a faith that can move mountains, but have not love, I am nothing. If I give all I possess to the poor and surrender my body to the flames, but have not love, I gain nothing.* 1 Corinthians 13:1-3

God *gave* Randy all the gifts and abilities that make him successful and popular: his quick mind, his outgoing personality, his ability to communicate. And of course God wants Randy to use the gifts he gave. But God isn't impressed with Randy's success. He says all those accomplishments are for nothing without love.

What are two areas in which you feel successful?

_____

_____

What motivates you in those areas of accomplishments? Peer pressure? Perfectionism? Love?

_____

_____

Examine the consistency of your love for people and your motives for succeeding. Remember—God doesn't beat around the bush when it comes to love:

> *Anyone who does not do what is right is not a child of God; nor is anyone who does not love his brother. This is the message you heard from the beginning: We should love one another.* 1 John 3:10b-11.

☐ DAY TWO

Summer Vacation

When Carrie's older sister, Meg, came home from college the summer after her freshman year, Carrie was shocked. Meg was so different! *Whatever it is they did to her at college*, Carrie thought, *I like it!*

Instead of spreading her piles of junk beyond her half of the room and onto Carrie's side, Meg apologized for being such a slob all the time and promised to work at keeping it clean.

Instead of making Carrie grovel before loaning her any clothes, Meg offered them! And she made a big deal of helping Carrie get dressed and fix her hair before a date.

Instead of ignoring her sister to go shopping with her college friends, Meg actually invited Carrie to come along. "We won't tell them how old you are!" she laughed.

Instead of bragging about all her college-life freedoms and privileges, she listened to Carrie talk about high school, struggles with Dad, and hopes for the future.

Carrie couldn't believe the change in Meg!

What Happened to You?

Finally Carrie had to ask, "What happened to make you so different, Meg?"

You can probably guess Meg's answer. She'd met a lot of Christian students at college, and eventually she'd met Christ, too.

Carrie's mouth dropped open in surprise when she saw Meg take a blue Bible out from under her pillow. Meg opened the book to a passage she had marked:

> *Love is patient, love is kind. It does not envy, it does not boast, it is not proud.* 1 Corinthians 13:4

Carrie read the words and nodded her head. *Yep—those words describe the new Meg*, she thought. *Maybe this Christianity stuff is for real.*

The Love Factor

Meg's loving behavior in her life at home could be an important factor for introducing Carrie to God's love. Her behavior was so different, Carrie had to ask, "What happened to you?"

Does your love give evidence of Christ living in you?

_____

_____

Do you think your family members credit your loving actions to your status as a child of God?

_____

_____

Ask God now to give you a faithful love that reminds people—especially those people who live at your house!—of his Son.

☐ DAY THREE

Flunking Math— On Purpose

Matt got up on the wrong side of the bed!

It all began when his dad got up at 5:30 a.m. to ride his exercise bike before getting ready for work. Matt's alarm was set for 7:00 a.m., but the noise outside his door kept him awake and grumbling under the covers. *One,* he counted, *the first annoyance of the day.*

Matt's sister Mindy took an extra-long time in the bathroom, and Matt had to wait. *Two!* he frowned, as he waited in the hallway. When he finally did get into the bathroom, he burned his arm on Mindy's curling iron, which she'd forgotten to turn off—again. *That's three!*

There was no milk for his Frosted Flakes, so he had to have toast for breakfast. And Mom had packed him a bag lunch again, even though he'd told her a million times that it was embarrassing to bring a brown bag when everyone else bought lunch at school or went out to McDonald's. *Four, Five!* he kept on counting.

Dad had left for the office early, not realizing Matt's chemistry textbook was on the floor of the backseat. And he hadn't offered Matt a ride to school, so Matt would have to ride the bus. *Six, seven!*

Matt was really getting mad. Already seven infractions on his personal rights, and it was only 8:00 in the morning!

Boy, Matt thought, *my family must lay awake nights thinking up ways to pick on me. And they expect me to go out of my way and do*

dishes and run errands and rake leaves after the way they treat me.
Well, they can just forget it!

It Doesn't Add Up

Matt has a problem with math—he's too good at it! He'd feel a
lot better and be a lot better off if he'd quit adding up the nega-
tives about his family.

Here's what Paul said about love in 1 Corinthians:

> *It [love] is not rude, it is not self-seeking, it is not easily an-*
> *gered, it keeps no record of wrongs.* 1 Corinthians 13:5

Matt's habit of counting up "wrongs" is a "self-seeking" habit that
makes him "easily angered." It's a habit that doesn't add up to
love.

How's Your Bookkeeping?

Does someone in your family have an irritating habit that you're
keeping close track of?

_____

_____

Does this kind of "record of wrongs" help you feel patient and
loving—or impatient and fed up—with that person?

_____

_____

Ask God to give you a lousy memory when it comes to "wrongs."
Ask him to keep you from being "self-seeking." Remember—God
is the source of the kind of love that covers wrongs.

> *Above all, love each other deeply, because love covers over a*
> *multitude of sins.* 1 Peter 4:8

☐ DAY FOUR

Not for Quitters

I have a friend who got pregnant during her senior year of high school. I'll call her Tanya for now.

Tanya is a Christian, and her parents and younger brother are Christians, too. Needless to say, Tanya was *terrified* to tell her family about the trouble she was in.

True Love

Tanya told her mom first, bracing herself for the anger and hysterics she felt sure would come. But Tanya and her mother ended up crying together, and Tanya felt relieved to have gotten the problem out in the open. "I'll help you talk with Dad about it," her mom offered. "We'll tell him together after church tomorrow."

Tanya sat between her parents during church the next morning. Her heart ached as she imagined her dad's hurt and disappointment when she'd tell him she was pregnant. During the sermon her father smiled at her lovingly and held her hand for awhile. Tanya felt like her heart would break. Telling him would be so hard!

But when dinner was over and she joined her parents in the living room, her dad said, "Tanya, Mom told me last night." And Tanya cried again because her dad had treated her with such tenderness just that morning even though he knew!

The Promise and the Plan

They told Tanya's brother, and together they made a family pact that none of them would ever, *ever* tell about Tanya's pregnancy unless Tanya wanted to tell. And then they came up with a plan to send Tanya to stay with a friend in the next state during the pregnancy. She'd leave about the same time her friends left for college. This way, Tanya's move wouldn't seem strange to her friends and relatives.

So Tanya went to stay with a warm-hearted older lady for several months. Her family visited and called frequently, and Tanya took two college courses and made homemade Christmas presents for each member of her family.

Her parents left the decision up to her, and Tanya chose to allow her baby to be adopted by a Christian family. It was a hard time for all of them, but her family had a love that wouldn't quit. They kept living out a pattern of protective, hopeful, persevering love.

> *Love does not delight in evil but rejoices with the truth. It always protects, always trusts, always hopes, always perseveres.*
> 1 Corinthians 13:6-7

Love Made the Difference

Tanya does tell some people her story. Her grandparents know, and of course I know—or I couldn't be telling it to you. Sometimes Tanya tells about her experience because she thinks it might help some other girl facing the same dilemma.

Tanya is a great girl—happy, creative, popular, and loving. The stage was set for disaster, but the supportive love of her family made the difference.

How tough and flexible is your love for your family members?

_____

_____

Take an honest look at your love. Is it the kind of love that's not for quitters? Could it weather a crisis like Tanya's family's love did?

_____

_____

Ask God now for a love that always protects, always trusts, always hopes, and always perseveres.

☐ DAY FIVE

Love Like Superglue

Amanda's sister Regina had finally run away for the last time. Regina had run away before, but never so far away (three whole states) and never for so long (nearly seven months). Amanda didn't think Regina would be back.

Regina's trouble had started with failing grades, some drinking, and a few wild friends. The trouble led to deceiving Amanda and their mom, a drug problem, and eventually long periods away from home.

Tough Love

Amanda and her mom tried to keep the lines of communication open with Regina. They kept her room ready for her, they sent some money, and they spent long hours on the phone. Their love for Regina kept on forgiving, and Regina had to know that their love was sticking like superglue: strong and permanent.

At the end of their last conversation with Regina, Amanda and her mom were each listening on one extension of the phone. Amanda heard her mother say, "We love you so much, Regina!"

And Amanda heard her sister whisper, just before she hung up, "I know it, Mom, I know."

Love Never Fails

"Love never fails" is another part of the message of 1 Corinthians 13 (verse 8). Here's a great story from the Bible that draws a picture of God's superglue kind of love.

There was a man who had two sons. The younger one said to his father, "Father, give me my share of the estate." So he divided his property between them.

Not long after that, the younger son got together all he had, set off for a distant country and there squandered his wealth in wild living. After he had spent everything, there was a severe famine in that whole country, and he began to be in need. So he went and hired himself out to a citizen of that country, who sent him to his fields to feed pigs. He longed to fill his stomach with the pods that the pigs were eating, but no one gave him anything.

When he came to his senses, he said, "How many of my father's hired men have food to spare, and here I am starving to death! I will set out and go back to my father and say to him: Father, I have sinned against heaven and against you. I am no longer worthy to be called your son; make me like one of your hired men." So he got up and went to his father.

But while he was still a long way off, his father saw him and was filled with compassion for him; he ran to his son, threw his arms around him and kissed him.

The son said to him, "Father, I have sinned against heaven and against you. I am no longer worthy to be called your son."

But the father said to his servants, "Quick! Bring the best robe and put it on him. Put a ring on his finger and sandals on his feet. Bring the fatted calf and kill it. Let's have a feast and celebrate. Luke 15:11-23

It's the Greatest

Do you love your family with God's brand of love, a superglue kind? What are some ways you can show that love this week?

_____

_____

_____

Ask God to help you grow in love for your family. Ask him to fill you up with his love for each one of them.

> *Now these three remain: faith, hope and love. But the greatest of these is love.* 1 Corinthians 13:13

Brothers and Sisters

☐ DAY ONE

Keeping
Secrets

W hen Max got home from his date on Friday night (just in time for his 12:30 curfew), his parents were still up, waiting and talking together in the living room. Max's brother, Jim, was still out. Max said goodnight and headed for bed. As he went down the hall, he heard his parents praying for Jim and thought he heard his mother crying.

To Talk or Not to Talk

Max knew the reason for his parents' concern and his mom's tears. Jim had been increasingly away from home and more and more difficult to live with when he was there. Jim's grades were dropping and he seemed uneasy. They brought it up, but Jim didn't seem to want to talk about whatever was troubling him.

Max thought he knew something more. Although Jim was a year older, Max knew that he hung out with Marty—and everyone knew Marty took drugs. The week before, Max had passed Jim in the hall just as Jim took something from Marty and stuffed it in his locker. *Drugs*, Max thought. *My brother is doing drugs.*

Max and Jim had always been close—at least until lately. Over the years they'd shared lots of secrets, never tattling on each other to the folks when one of them got in trouble at school. One year Max even hid his report card for two weeks because Jim didn't want to show his to their parents. But now Max was starting to wonder, are some secrets bad secrets? When is helping not helping anymore?

Max was tired from a long week at school and his night out, but he couldn't get to sleep. Should he tell his parents about Jim's problem?

What Do You Think?

Maybe you have a sister or brother (or good friend) who does drugs. Or maybe it's a different problem, like anorexia, drinking too much, or cheating. How are you handling it now? Have you told anyone else about the problem? Write about it here.

_____

_____

_____

If you were in Max's spot, what would you do?

_____

_____

When You Don't Know What to Do

The Book of James has some good advice for those times when you just don't know what to do.

> *Consider it pure joy, my brothers, whenever you face trials of many kinds, because you know that the testing of your faith develops perseverance. Perseverance must finish its work so that you may be mature and complete, not lacking in anything. If any of you lacks wisdom, he should ask God, who gives generously to all without finding fault, and it will be given to him.* James 1:2-5

What a promise! If we lack wisdom, we don't have to be ashamed. We simply ask God—he's promised to give it.

Right now, ask God for wisdom in handling the problem you wrote about above. Thank him for his promise of help!

☐ DAY TWO

After the Lights Go Out

Susan turned out the lamp by her bed and lay in the dark, but she was too angry to sleep. She could hear her sister, Sarah, crying softly into her pillow, but she really didn't care. They were both grounded, and it was all Sarah's fault.

Earlier that afternoon Sarah had talked Susan into going with her to the mall. They had promised to be home in time to help Mom make dinner, since the pastor and his wife were coming over. Susan should have known that Sarah would ditch her at the mall to go hang out with her best friend Brenda and some boys—all Sarah wanted Susan for was her driver's license! Sarah hadn't shown up to go home when she was supposed to, and Susan had waited for her. By the time they got home, dinner had already started, and Mom was really mad.

"It's always been this way with her," thought Susan. "Even when we were little she was getting me into trouble." Susan remembered when Sarah had used a crayon to spell out Susan's name on the playroom wall; of course, Susan was blamed for the mess. And she thought of all the times Sarah borrowed her clothes without returning them clean and ironed. *I know I'm supposed to love my sister,* she thought, *but I don't know how much forgiveness I have left in me.*

Put on Love

Susan is really frustrated, and you can't blame her for feeling that Sarah's chances at forgiveness should have run out long ago. So how does a person who feels pushed to the limit obey the command of Colossians 3:13-14?

> *Bear with each other and forgive whatever grievances you may have against one another. Forgive as the Lord forgave you. And over all these virtues, put on love, which binds them all together in perfect unity.*

The verse commands us to forgive in the same way that God forgave us. In God's eyes, we're like Sarah, repeatedly selfish, disobedient, and insensitive—always requiring forgiveness. But God provided the ultimate forgiveness in the person of Christ who died for all our sins, past and present. The Bible says that when we confess our sins, God takes them as far as the east is from the west and he remembers them no more. Now that's forgive and forget!

Susan may not naturally feel forgiving toward her sister, but God can give her a supernatural dose of love for Sarah to help her keep on forgiving.

Can you think of someone in your family who you really need to forgive? Write about the problem here:

_____

_____

Ask God to fill you up with forgiveness. He can give you the kind of love that helps you forgive before the lights go out!

> *In your anger do not sin: Do not let the sun go down while you are still angry.* Ephesians 4:26

☐ DAY THREE

Eating
Dust

When Reuben was eight and his sister, Rosa, was ten, they looked just like twins. Rosa was rather rowdy for a girl, and Reuben didn't mind playing "girls' games" now and then, so things evened out somewhere in the middle, and they were best pals. They climbed trees, made forts in their bedroom closets, and played school in the back yard.

And part of being best pals was keeping each other in line. The first time Rosa caught her little brother using bad words, she knocked him down in the dirt of the playground and pushed his face in the dust 'til he promised he'd never do it again. Maybe her punishment was a little rough, but her heart was in the right place. She just wanted her best pal to be *good*.

Keeping Each Other in Line

Rosa and Reuben still keep each other in line. Reuben tells Rosa when he thinks she's being too hard on their other brother. Rosa tells Reuben when she thinks he's not treating their mom with consideration. And sometimes they get mad at each other. After all, nobody likes to hear about his own faults.

But Rosa and Reuben are best pals. Reuben knows his big sister loves him, so it's a little bit easier to take when she makes him "eat dust." And Rosa knows her brother just wants her to be the best that she can be.

Brothers and sisters and parents are in a unique position for helping each other love and serve the Lord. Those people you live with know your faults, but they love you, too. And it's a lot easier to take criticism (or rebuke) from someone who cares about you.

> *Better is open rebuke*
> *than hidden love.*
> *Wounds from a friend can be trusted.* Proverbs 27:5-6a

> *As iron sharpens iron,*
> *so one man sharpens another.* Proverbs 27:17

Has one of your family members ever tried to talk to you about something you did that bothered or hurt him? How did it turn out? Were you angry? Did you think your brother or sister or parent was right? Write about it briefly.

_____

_____

_____

What do you think would happen if you talked to a brother or a sister (or a close friend) about something you feel they've done wrong? Would your sister or brother know that you loved her or him by the way you explained the problem? Write about it.

_____

_____

_____

Before you ever try to talk with a family member about a problem, pray! Pray now, asking God to give you wisdom and love that will help you be a faithful, truthful member of your family.

And if it happens to be your turn to "eat dust," pray and ask God to help you take the criticism and encouragement well. Ask God now to help your family be "iron sharpening iron," making one another sharp for service to him.

☐ DAY FOUR

Margie and Mel

*L*ucky me, thought Margie, as she pasted on a phony smile. The pastor's wife meant well, of course, but Margie wanted to puke every time someone said, "You're so lucky to have a sister like Melanie!"

Mel got straight *A's*, sang hymns in the shower, actually enjoyed doing the dishes, and had recently finished reading her Bible straight through in one year.

Margie, on the other hand, doodled on her classnotes, had a voice like a moose with laryngitis, felt sick when it came to housework, liked romance novels, and often sneaked out to go dancing when she was supposed to be at the library.

Oh, lucky me! she thought. *I always suffer in comparison . . .*

Gag Me!

Before you feel like smacking Melanie and gagging yourself along with Margie, walk in Melanie's tennis shoes for a minute.

Last week Peter Schmidt—tall, blonde, and athletic— stopped Mel in the hallway after church to ask her if she was still planning to be out of town with her family that weekend.

This is it! thought Melanie. *He's finally going to ask me out!* She crossed her fingers and answered him.

"Grandma's sick, so we're not going this weekend."

"Great!" he replied. "I'm going to see if Margie wants to go to the football game with me."

Melanie held back the tears. *Of course—Margie*. When Margie smiled, every guy in the room watched her face. And Margie was fun! The crowd always followed her, and she made them laugh and thought up great things to do. Mel would give almost everything to be as pretty and lighthearted as Margie.

Just Like Her

Wouldn't each of these girls be surprised to discover how much her sister envied her? It sounds like both girls are good at being who they are. Maybe they just don't see the good stuff in themselves because they're so busy trying to measure up to somebody else's measuring stick.

Name two characteristics of one of your sisters or brothers (or a parent) that you wish you had:

_____

_____

You were "fearfully and wonderfully made" by the Lord—Psalm 139 says so. You were planned from the color of your hair to the sound of your laugh to the way you relate to people. God knew what you would be like, and he takes pleasure in his creation—you. He cares for you every minute of your life, and his thoughts are always with you.

> *I praise you because I am fearfully and wonderfully made;*
> *your works are wonderful,*
> *I know that full well.*
> *My frame was not hidden from you*
> *when I was made in that secret place.*
> *When I was woven together in the depths of the earth,*
> *your eyes saw my unformed body.*
> *All the days ordained for me*
> *were written in your book*
> *before one of them came to be.*
> *How precious to me are your thoughts, O God!*
> *How vast is the sum of them!*

Were I to count them,
  they would outnumber the grains of sand.
Psalm 139:14-18

What are some things that you like about yourself? Name as many as you can (at least four):

_____

_____

_____

_____

Thank the Lord now for making you the way he did. Celebrate what God created when he created you. Thank him, too, for making each of your family members unique.

☐ DAY FIVE

Lifetime Guarantee

My family moved about eleven or twelve (or was it thirteen?) times during the years before I went away to college. In each new place we made good friends, but it took awhile. So every time we moved I thanked God that I had brothers and sisters. It gave me someone to play with or hang out with until I made some friends.

I didn't think about my brothers and sisters in the same category as my friends—you probably don't either. But one day when I started to think about it, I realized, "Hey—I like these people. I bet I'd even like them if they weren't in my family and I'd just met them at school!" It was a great discovery.

Friends Forever

You know how they say, "Blood is thicker than water"? Well, it's true. Hopefully during your lifetime you will make some friends who are true blue, the kind of friends that will stick by you until you're in the old folks' home together, playing shuffleboard and talking about old times. But many of your friendships won't last that long—for lots of different reasons. Maybe your values and personality will change. Maybe your friend's will. Maybe you'll go away to college and never move back to your home state. Or maybe your friend will move. Maybe you'll have six kids someday, and your best friend will be jetsetting around the world in an absorbing career. There's no telling. And it's exciting to wonder how our lives and friendships will unfold.

But no matter what other things change, your flesh-and-blood family will always be *your family*. The friendships you develop with your brothers and sisters are lifetime-guarantee friendships.

It Makes a Difference

It makes a difference to think about your family members as forever friends. In the middle of your next fight over a TV program, watch what you say! Ten years down the road, you may not remember what the fight was about, but you'll remember the hurtful words you spoke to one another.

Maybe knowing that your sister or brother is going to be your lifelong friend will make you want to work at that friendship more. Look for the things you like about your brother. Once in a while, go to the mall with your sister instead of your best friend. Invest some time and energy into that long-lasting friendship.

How good and pleasant it is when brothers live together in unity! Psalm 133:1

We love because he first loved us. If anyone says, "I love God," yet hates his brother, he is a liar. For anyone who does not love his brother, whom he has seen, cannot love God, whom he has not seen. And he has given us this command: Whoever loves God must also love his brother. 1 John 4:19-21

Self-Check

What about you? Do your actions and attitudes at home demonstrate your lifetime-guarantee friendship to your brothers and sisters?

What are two practical ways you can show your love to a sister or brother today?

_____

_____

_____

Ask God to give you creative ideas for building friendships in your family. Ask him to fill you up with his love for your brothers and sisters so that you will be the best possible friend to them.

Talk, Talk, Talk

☐ DAY ONE

Table Talk

On the TV show "Growing Pains," the TV dad gets his family together on a boat, steers the boat far from shore, then steals the sparkplug from the motor. He's desperately trying to find a way to get his family to talk to each other. It's rather sneaky and underhanded, but it works—at least for awhile.

But that's TV—a Hollywood family. Things are much tougher in real families. Dads work, Moms often work, and the kids are in school and sports and choir and everything else. Most families are doing great if they all make it home for dinner each night!

And getting home is just the beginning. Each person is busy thinking about his or her own thing. Mom, a lawyer, has a headache because of a difficult day in court. Dad is a social worker, and he comes home very worried about a client with troubles. Frank is bone-tired after a long afternoon of track practice and has to spend the evening cramming for a history exam. Mindy's best friend is gossiping about her around school, and Mindy can't think of anything else except how hurt she feels. How on earth can a family bring so many different feelings and interests together to have a *real* conversation?

It Takes Work

Communication takes work. It means taking the headphones all the way off (instead of lifting them off one ear) when Mom is talking to you, just to show her you really care about what she says. It means calling home to tell your parents where you are and when you'll be home. It means inconveniencing yourself for the sake of the whole team—your family. It means setting *your* interests and feelings aside for a bit to concentrate on those other people who live in your house!

Paul's words to the Philippians are a helpful encouragement:

Do nothing out of selfish ambition or vain conceit, but in humility consider others better than yourselves. Each of you should look not only to your own interests, but also to the interests of others. Philippians 2:3-4

Who knows? With a little effort, this family's dinner could turn into an encouragement session. Frank notices that Mindy seems upset and asks her about her problem. Mom notices the tired-looking sag in Frank's shoulders and finds out that she can help by quizzing Frank from his history book. Mindy realizes that Mom isn't feeling well and offers to do the dishes so that Mom can put her feet up after dinner. The family shows an interest in Dad's troubled client, and they pray together, helping their father bring his work to the Lord. Wow! A lot can happen when you start "looking to the interests of others" in your family.

What are some communication needs in your family?

_____

_____

Ask the Lord to help you communicate in your family. Ask him to help you put aside your own concerns to listen to them. Write the name of one family member you will take special time to listen to and talk with today:

_____

☐ DAY TWO

I'm Rubber and You're Glue

When I was in the ninth grade, my family lived within walking distance of my school. The walk was a straight half-mile of sidewalk that ran along behind the backyards of another neighborhood.

One day I was walking home alone, and I noticed a guy working in his yard. He looked just a few years older than I. He noticed me, too, and walked over to the fence. Leaning over the edge he said, "Gosh—you're ugly!"

Ouch! That one really hurt.

Dishing It Out

I'm no beauty queen, but I didn't deserve such a nasty comment—especially from someone I didn't even know.

It hurts even more coming from someone you love. I remember my brothers teasing, "When you go down to the wharf, not even the tugboats whistle!" I knew they didn't mean it, but I didn't forget either.

And I did my share of dishing it out! I'd pull on my brother's nose and call it his "beak"—even though it's really not that big. And I teased him mercilessly about not having any muscles—when he was really too young to have any! (He's big and muscular now, so I guess the joke's on me.)

Sticks and Stones

"Sticks and stones may break my bones, but words will never hurt me," we'd chant in a singsong voice. Or, "I'm rubber and you're glue; what you say bounces off me and sticks on you," as if we really believed we could send the hurtful words back to the one who said them.

Those rhymes are kid stuff. You and I both know—from experience—that painful words seem to stick forever to influence the way we feel about ourselves and that the encouraging words we receive seem to go in one ear and out the other before we even begin to believe them.

Zip Your Lip

Try to remember a time when you said something less than kind to a member of your family. It probably wasn't too long ago! Write about it here.

_____

_____

> *Therefore, as God's chosen people, holy and dearly loved, clothe yourselves with compassion, kindness, humility, gentleness and patience.* Colossians 3:12
>
> *Do not let any unwholesome talk come out of your mouths, but only what is helpful for building others up according to their needs, that it may benefit those who listen. And do not grieve the Holy Spirit of God, with whom you were sealed for the day of redemption.* Ephesians 4:29-30

Ask God two things today. First, ask him to forgive you for all the times you can remember speaking hurtful words to a member of your family. Then ask God to help you guard your tongue to keep it from doing damage to the people you love.

Thank him for his forgiveness and his help!

☐ DAY THREE

Big Mouth

S erena had a big mouth. She knew it, and she was sorry about it. Night after night she'd go to bed realizing that she'd blown it again: criticizing her brother's computerized windmill science project, slipping her sister's secret into Mom's ear, or hogging the conversation at dinner.

Why didn't all her resolutions and good intentions work?!

Serena's Strategy

Serena finally talked with her mom about the problem, and her mom suggested that she read the Book of Proverbs and copy all the verses that refer to the tongue or talking.

This is ridiculous, thought Serena once she got started. *There must be a hundred of these!*

There were so many it took her nearly a month to finish the project. These are a few of the verses she wrote down:

The tongue that brings healing is a tree of life. Proverbs 15:4

A man finds joy in giving an apt reply—and how good is a timely word! Proverbs 15:23

A wise man's heart guides his mouth, and his lips promote instruction. Pleasant words are a honeycomb, sweet to the soul and healing to the bones. Proverbs 16:23-24

Curse or Blessing?

Pretty soon Serena started to realize that with some self-control and the help of the Holy Spirit, her big-mouth curse could actually become a blessing.

Her infamous gift of gab was useful for keeping her bedridden Grandpa company.

She discovered that she could be a great friend to shy people.

Her creative ability for clever put-downs against her sister and brother was really just the flip side of a creative ability to encourage and build up others. It became a challenge—and a sharpening skill—always to find something nice to say.

That's the Way God Made Her

After all, who gave Serena her motor mouth? God did! And he was just waiting for Serena to dig into his Word to discover how to use her "gift" for his kingdom.

Make a list of your immediate family members. After each name, write down one praiseworthy item about that person.

    Name   *Positive characteristic*

_____   _____

_____   _____

_____   _____

Do you have a "gift" that can be both a curse and a blessing? Write down some ideas for how you can use that gift to please God.

_____

_____

_____

Ask God to help you communicate your encouraging words to your family today. (Sometimes this is very difficult!) Ask him to teach you through his Word how to use all your gifts for him.

☐ DAY FOUR

Take It Back!

One Saturday afternoon during my sophomore year of high school, my older brother, Marc, and I fought a verbal World War III while my parents weren't home.

I don't remember who started it or exactly what we were fighting about, but I do remember saying, "I can't wait until you leave—maybe we'll be a real family then!"

Bite My Tongue

I'm ashamed of those words now, but my heart was pretty hard back then. My brother was a senior and was planning to join the Navy soon after graduation. I was looking forward to being the new "oldest" of us kids, and I was sick of fighting with him.

It's true that things were a bit quieter without him. After all, there was one less person to share the phone, the bathroom, and our parents' car with! There was one less person to get in my way when I was grouchy.

But the words I'd said kept hanging out in the corners of my mind. I'd been wrong—our family wasn't "better" without Marc. Instead we had a big hole where he should've been. I hoped he wasn't far away from us at boot camp remembering my hateful shouts and thinking his nasty little sister didn't love and miss him. How I wished I could take those angry words back!

75

Lifelong Challenge

Controlling my tongue is my lifelong challenge. I've always had a careless, selfish habit of blabbing first and regretting it later.

The Book of James teaches about the importance of taming the tongue:

> *If anyone is never at fault in what he says, he is a perfect man, able to keep his whole body in check.*
>
> *When we put bits into the mouths of horses to make them obey us, we can turn the whole animal. Or take ships as an example. Although they are so large and are driven by strong winds, they are steered by a very small rudder wherever the pilot wants to go. Likewise the tongue is a small part of the body, but it makes great boasts. Consider what a great forest is set on fire by a small spark. The tongue also is a fire, a world of evil among the parts of the body. It corrupts the whole person, sets the whole course of his life on fire, and is itself set on fire by hell. . . .*
>
> *With the tongue we praise our Lord and Father, and with it we curse men, who have been made in God's likeness. Out of the same mouth come praise and cursing. My brothers, this should not be.* James 3:2b-6, 9-10

Double Talk

How can hateful, ugly words come out of the same mouth that says, "I love you and will serve you, Lord!"? That's hypocritical. Blessing and cursing from the same mouth is disgusting to God. The tongue is such a little part of the body, but what trouble it can cause!

What about you? Do you struggle with controlling your tongue? Remember the last time you said something you wished you could take back? Write about it here.

_____

_____

_____

Is there something you can do to help the person you hurt? Write down your ideas.

_____

_____

Be honest with God about your struggles with your tongue. Ask him to give you a spirit of self control and the strength it takes to control that powerful tongue.

Thank him for his enduring love and his ever-present help!

☐ DAY FIVE

Putting Your Heart on the Line

My sister Adele and I shared a room for years and years. So we had plenty of time to establish a regular fight pattern. First we'd freeze each other out. Our bedroom would be totally silent except for the deliberate slamming of dresser drawers and closet doors. We'd let each other know we were mad without speaking. Maybe Adele would kick my dirty clothes over onto my side of the room. Or I'd take any clothes I'd loaned her and move them—very obviously—back to my side of the closet.

Then one of us would speak up, and the verbal warfare began. Pretty soon Adele and I would be shouting or crying, and Mom would come in with her "I'm-so-disappointed-in-you-guys" face.

Mom, the Referee

Mom would make us sit next to each other on the living room couch, and she'd sit there with us to referee. Adele and I wouldn't be able to look each other in the face, so we'd both direct our conversation at Mom instead of at each other. And Mom wouldn't let us go until the anger was gone, and we were both really sorry.

Sometimes it took awhile, but usually Adele and I would end

up bawling like babies and hugging each other and vowing we'd
never fight like that again.

A Better Way

Adele and I would both have been a lot better off if one of us had
had the guts to speak up about our hurt or angry feelings *before*
beginning the knock-down-drag-out fight.

But it takes a lot of courage to say without anger, "You hurt
my feelings when you said . . ." or "It bothers me when you . . ."

Telling the truth in love is part of God's plan for getting
along in our immediate families and in the family of God.

> *I urge you to live a life worthy of the calling you have received.
> Be completely humble and gentle; be patient, bearing with one
> another in love. Make every effort to keep the unity of the Spir-
> it through the bond of peace. . .*
>
> *Speaking the truth in love, we will in all things grow up
> into him who is the Head, that is, Christ. From him the whole
> body, joined and held together by every supporting ligament,
> grows and builds itself up in love, as each part does its work.*
> Ephesians 4:1-3, 15-16

Switching Gears

Adele and I have been growing in the Lord. It's been years since
I've seen any trace of the old fight pattern. But it still isn't easy to
talk to each other about things that hit close to home. Putting our
hearts on the line is always a discipline.

Describe any fight patterns you see at your house.

_____

_____

_____

Could these patterns be reversed by "speaking the truth in love"?

_____

_____

Ask God to give you the guts to talk about the *truth*—about feelings of hurt or anger. Ask him to give you a spirit of love and peace.

Family Reunion

☐ DAY ONE

Heroes

E verybody has a hero—a youth pastor, a teacher, a politician, musician, or TV star. Very often a hero is a parent or another close relative. It makes sense—after all we spend a lot of time with those people!

My parents are two of my heroes. I want to work hard with integrity for the kingdom of God—like my Dad does. I want to be patient and sensitive like Mom.

Fill in this chart about your heroes.

Hero	What I Like About Him/Her
_____	_____
_____	_____
_____	_____

Beautiful But Dumb

For some reason, a beautiful and foolish girl named Salome looked up to her mother. Her mother, Herodias, was married to her uncle, King Herod. That arrangement was against God's law, but no one in the kingdom had the guts to accuse the king of sinning—except for righteous John the Baptist. And his courage landed him in prison. Herodias was pretty steamed.

One night Herod's important friends came over for a party. Everybody got drunk, and Herod himself was completely plastered. Herodias (not a nice lady at all) developed an evil plan for getting rid of that nuisance John the Baptist once and for all. Silly Salome just went along with everything Herodias told her to do.

What kind of mom sends her daughter to dance in front of drunk men? But that's what Herodias sent Salome to do. And Salome did such a good job of it that drunk old Herod hiccupped and offered anything she wanted, up to half the kingdom.

That kind of offer to a young girl was like a fairy godmother giving out free wishes. But Salome didn't ask for a Porsche, a new fall wardrobe, or a trust fund for her college education. She listened to her mother's evil influence and asked for John's head on a platter. And she got it, much to Herodias' delight.

We don't have any more information about Salome. But given the kind of person she looked up to, I doubt she turned out well.

Brains and Beauty Both

Esther was a gorgeous girl who picked the right kind of people to model herself after. When her parents died, Esther's cousin Mordecai gave her a home. He taught her to honor God and to serve God with her life. Esther learned to love and obey God mostly because she had such a great example in Mordecai, who served God and his king without seeking glory and riches for himself.

Esther turned out to be a beauty queen and eventually the Queen herself. And because of her position as Queen, she managed to save God's chosen people from a fiendish plot to wipe them out completely. She risked her life to follow Mordecai's instructions. God honored Mordecai's wisdom and Esther's obedience. Read the incredible story for yourself in the Book of Esther.

Everybody's Got Heroes

Everybody learns and grows by modeling after other people. That's the way God made us. Ask God to help you choose godly men and women as your models.

> *Above all, make Christ himself your model and example. Be imitators of God, therefore, as dearly loved children and live a life of love, just as Christ loved us* . . . Ephesians 5:1-2a

☐ DAY TWO

Rug
Rats

The door closed behind Aunt Betty and Uncle Dwayne, and Julia was alone with Petey and Jenna. *Rug rats!* she thought. *That's what Mark would call them if he were here.* She and her friend Mark would've gone out that night, but here she was at Grandpa's house, tending the babies while the adults went out to eat. She wasn't looking forward to this! Julia didn't like little kids very much.

Adventures in Babysitting

In a popular movie, a babysitter and some kids experience a night to remember. They have a blowout on the freeway, get rescued by a one-handed crazy man, dodge bullets in a shootout, ride in a stolen car, escape from sinister crooks, perform on stage in a nightclub, get caught in the middle of a gang war, and hang from the outside of a skyscraper.

Julia didn't have quite that much excitement, but she had a night to remember, too. By the end of the evening, Julia had decided that little kids were okay—at least, Petey and Jenna were.

Petey got a nosebleed, and Julia mopped him up and held him until the bleeding stopped. "I love you, Julie," he said, giving her a soft kiss on the cheek.

And even after her mom and dad came home, Jenna wouldn't go to sleep without a good-night hug from Julia.

Going Backward

Julia had forgotten how honest and affectionate little kids could be. Life was definitely less stressful when you didn't have to work at impressing people or play popularity games—Jenna and Peter's straightforward love was really refreshing.

You can't stay a kid forever, and God doesn't want you to. He wants you to take on the responsibilities and rewards of adult life. He wants you to grow into a mature relationship with him. But God has a special place in his heart for children, and in some ways teens and grown-ups need to go backward to reclaim an attitude of openness and willingness to trust in him.

> *"I tell you the truth, unless you change and become like little children, you will never enter the kingdom of heaven. Therefore, whoever humbles himself like this child is the greatest in the kingdom of heaven. And whoever welcomes a little child like this in my name welcomes me."* Matthew 18:3-5

> *Jesus said, "Let the little children come to me, and do not hinder them, for the kingdom of heaven belongs to such as these."* Matthew 19:14

The Kids in Your Life

Are there any kids in your life? Maybe you have younger brothers and sisters, or maybe you have nieces and nephews already. Maybe you babysit, or take your turn in the church nursery.

What was your last experience with a person under twelve?

_____

_____

What has been your attitude toward spending time with kids?

_____

_____

Ask God to help you learn to love children. Pray specifically for the little kids you know and spend time with. Ask God to help you learn about him through your time spent with children.

☐ DAY THREE

Family Resemblance

I'm short like my mom, but my face looks more like Dad's. I have a nose like Dad's, but my voice sounds like Mom's. Wherever I go people say to me, "Honey, you look just like your _____" (Mom or Dad—fill in the blank!). Sometimes I wonder which of them I *really* look like. Truth is, I look like both of them.

Hand-Me-Downs

Whose looks did you end up with? Are you glad?! (If you're adopted, you may be thinking these questions don't apply to you. But adopted kids often pick up mannerisms in voice and actions that look just like those of their adoptive parents!)

Parents and grandparents hand down more than just brown hair, blue eyes, big noses, ears that stick out, etc. Living in your family all these years, you may have picked up a whole system of values, a whole picture of the world, that is similar to that of your mom or dad or both.

Make a list of the positive characteristics of one of your parents (for example: loyal, great cook, responsible, good listener, etc.). Then put a yes or no in the "Me" column if you think you might have inherited that good quality.

Parent's Quality	Me
_____	_____
_____	_____
_____	_____
_____	_____
_____	

Rich Heritage

Timothy's mom and grandma loved the Lord. Though his dad was not a Christian, he was one of the very fortunate few who was taught from his babyhood to love and obey the Lord. Probably a lot of credit for Timothy's hard work and ministry for the Lord goes to his grandmother, Lois, and his mother, Eunice, who started him off with the Lord and helped him grow in God.

No matter when you got started in your relationship with the Lord, it's important to know that God gave you the parents you have in order to teach you some good things. In a letter to Timothy, Paul encourages him not to forget the principles of godliness those two great women taught him:

> _But as for you, continue in what you have learned and have become convinced of, because you know those from whom you learned it, and how from infancy you have known the holy Scriptures, which are able to make you wise for salvation through faith in Christ Jesus._ 2 Timothy 3:14-15

Thank God for the positive characteristics that you have inherited from your parent(s). Ask God to help you develop those good qualities so that you can use them to help others and serve him. Ask God to help you obey Paul's challenge to Timothy to be faithful in remembering and following the teaching of the Word of God.

☐ DAY FOUR

Dinner at Grandma's

"**A**gain?!" Sondra hollered. "Why do we have to spend every Sunday with Grandma, anyway?"

Sondra's family had a big Sunday brunch with her grandmother every Sunday after church. Sondra hadn't minded so much when she was a little kid—after all, Granny was a great cook and she had some cool toys in her basement. But now Sondra hated to miss the youth group softball game on Sunday afternoons, and sometimes she wished her grandma lived in another state!

Oldtimers

After dinner Sondra plopped down on the couch and picked up the newspaper. The section that was lying there was the weekly crossword puzzle. Just for fun, Sondra tried a few of the clues. A three-letter word for swamp? The french word for hat? She found she couldn't answer a single question. Yet her Grandma had almost completely filled in the top half of the chart of little squares.

Grandma is incredibly smart, Sondra realized. *Wow! I didn't know that!*

Maybe by the time Sondra has lived sixty-plus years, she'll be able to fill in the New York Times Crossword puzzle. A lot of wisdom and knowledge comes from living lots of years. It would probably be worth Sondra's while to invest some time and energy into getting to know her grandma, into finding out some of the exciting or learning experiences of her grandmother's life. Sondra's grandma is a walking resource of wisdom for living.

Advice from an Older Person

Remember your Creator
   in the days of your youth,
before the days of trouble come
   and the years approach when you will say,
   "I find no pleasure in them"—
before the sun and the light
   and the moon and the stars grow dark,
   and the clouds return after the rain;
when the keepers of the house tremble,
   and the strong men stoop,
when the grinders cease because they are few,
   and those looking through the windows grow dim;
when the doors to the street are closed
   and the sound of grinding fades;
when men rise up at the sound of birds,
   but all their songs grow faint;
when men are afraid of heights
   and of dangers in the streets;
when the almond tree blossoms
   and the grasshopper drags himself along
   and desire no longer is stirred.
Then man goes to his eternal home
   and mourners go about the streets.
Remember him—before the silver cord is severed,
   or the golden bowl is broken;
before the pitcher is shattered at the spring,
   or the wheel broken at the well,
and the dust returns to the ground it came from,
   and the spirit returns to God who gave it.
Ecclesiastes 12:1-7

This is a poem about old age. See if you can pick out the words that describe failing eyesight and hearing, loss of strength and ability to use arms and legs, loss of teeth, an inability to get up and go out, and finally the imagery about death.

Then focus on the advice the older person gives at the beginning and at the end of the poem: "Remember your Creator in the days of your youth." Youth—that's now for you.

What do you think is involved in "remembering your Creator"? Make a list of some actions and attitudes.

_____

_____

_____

Old Folks

No doubt you know some older folks—either your own grandparents, elderly family friends or neighbors, or people at your church. Do a self-check:

How much attention do you give those older people when you are with them?

_____

Have you ever learned something about life from an older person? Write about it here.

_____

_____

Ask God to give you a love for older people. Ask him to make you teachable so that you can learn from the old folks in your life.

☐ DAY FIVE

Skeletons in the Family Closet

eggy pulled the pillow up over her head, but she could still hear every word coming from the next room. She was trying to sleep on the living room couch at her grandma's house, while her parents and aunts and uncles were sitting around the dining room table talking about old times.

At first they were laughing and joking in there, but now the voices were growing solemn and soft. Peggy was curious, wondering what juicy information the old folks revealed after she and the other cousins went to bed.

So Peggy pulled the pillow down again and strained her ears to hear the family secrets.

Eavesdropping

Peggy acquired a lot of new information that night.

The folks were talking about an uncle she couldn't remember ever seeing. They mentioned how the man had beaten her aunt Darla and mistreated his children, finally leaving Darla to raise the kids alone without any financial support. Peggy had never really thought about her missing uncle before; suddenly her aunt seemed to be an amazing and courageous woman.

And they talked about her grandfather, too. Peggy had known him as a kindhearted, gruff man in the years before his death. But her dad and his family could remember the days before he'd received Christ—days in which he drank heavily and was rough with his children.

What a lot of dirty laundry our family has! Peggy thought in surprise.

The Good Stuff

Then Peggy heard her father's voice again. He was explaining that because of those tough childhood experiences, he prayed every day asking God to make him a loving, gentle father to his own kids. "I'm thankful for those hard times now," he said. "Now I know that I can't be the best father without God's help to control my temper."

It's true, thought Peggy. *He does work hard to keep his cool when things go wrong at home.* And she was glad to know that her dad was trying so hard—for her.

And Aunt Darla was thanking God for her years of struggle, too. Because of those hard times, Aunt Darla had become a Christian. "The rough times come, but I know God is faithful," she was saying.

Peggy eventually drifted off to sleep, thanking God for her family—the bad stuff and the good stuff.

> *And we know that in all things God works for the good of those who love him, who have been called according to his purpose.*
> Romans 8:28

> *"Come, let us return to the LORD. He has torn us to pieces but he will heal us; he has injured us but he will bind up our wounds. After two days he will revive us; on the third day he will restore us, that we may live in his presence. Let us acknowledge the LORD; let us press on to acknowledge him. As surely as the sun rises, he will appear; he will come to us like the winter rains, like the spring rains that water the earth."*
> Hosea 6:1-3

Are there some painful secrets—past or present—in your family? Have you ever felt "torn to pieces" by a family situation? Write about it here.

_____

_____

_____

Have you seen any evidence of God's hand in those circumstances?

_____

_____

_____

Talk with God about the problem areas you wrote about. Ask him
to make those hard circumstances work for good in the lives of
you and your family members. Ask him to refresh you "like the
spring rains that water the earth."

All in the Family

☐ DAY ONE

Waving the White Flag

L aura sat on the edge of her brother's waterbed. "Justin," she said, poking his tennis shoe. Justin kept reading his comic book and ignored her.

Laura was on a mission of peace. Her sister Melissa was crying in their room down the hall, upset after a loud and angry argument with Justin.

"Justin, I think she's sorry now," Laura continued. Justin blinked and looked up at her. "She was grouchy anyway, Justin. She had a terrible day at school. I don't think she meant to take it out on you."

"O.K.," Justin replied, going back to his comics.

Laura sighed and wondered if her peacemaking efforts were worth anything. She got up to leave Justin's room. "I've got to get some Kleenex for 'Lissa—she looks terrible," she said.

As Laura was going out the door, Justin called after her, "Take mine!" And he tossed a box of Kleenex toward the door.

Laura smiled.

Blessed Are . . .

Once I got really furious with my dad and stormed off to my bedroom to bawl in private. And Mom came after me to talk. I really expected her to get on my case for talking back to Dad, but she didn't.

Instead she started telling me about all the things she valued in my Dad. Sneaky, huh? She was reminding me of all the things I really loved about him. My mom is a pretty good peacemaker.

> *"Blessed are the peacemakers, for they will be called sons of God."* Matthew 5:9

> *For where you have envy and selfish ambition, there you will find disorder and every evil practice.*
> *But the wisdom that comes from heaven is first of all pure; then peace-loving, considerate, submissive, full of mercy and good fruit, impartial and sincere. Peacemakers who sow in peace raise a harvest of righteousness.* James 3:16-18

Mission—Impossible?

Ha! you're probably thinking. *You'd have to wear black and white stripes and blow a giant whistle to referee in my family!*

Be realistic. You're not going to be able to make peace between all the members of your family. But you can be a peaceful influence in your family by making peace and reconciliation your goal.

Start with yourself. Is there someone in your family you need to "make peace" with? Write out some ideas for how you can wave the white flag of surrender in that relationship.

_____

_____

_____

Remember—God specializes in impossible missions. Nothing is too hard for him. Ask him to bring peace to your home. Ask him to make you a peacemaker.

☐ DAY TWO

Perfect
or a Pain?

"**O**h, I could never be as perfect as you!" Ouch! Whoever said, "The truth hurts!" was right. Of course I wasn't perfect—and probably no one (except God) knows that better than my sister. She had to share a room with me for years and years! But she was telling me that I had pushed her too hard, that I had pressured her to be like me instead of like herself.

I still do that sometimes, but I'm learning not to. My sister has abilities and gifts that I appreciate so much—now that I'm not so hung up on my way of doing things. Looking back to when we were kids, I realize now that I was often a real pain in the neck.

Another Pain in the Neck

Joseph was a really fabulous guy. He trusted God through thick (being his dad's favorite boy, moving to the top in every job he landed in, living in luxury in a king's palace) and thin (abandonment, slavery, prison), and he ended up saving his family and millions of others from starving during a famine.

A guy like that doesn't sound like a pain in the neck. But if you had asked his older brothers back in the years when Joseph was living with the family, you would have heard a different story.

"Arrogant!"

"Too good for the rest of us!"

"Daddy's boy!"

"Brown-noser!"

It's not that Joseph was really so bad; the boys just didn't try very hard to understand each other, and dad's favoritism didn't help the situation much. Their family problem got so bad they eventually dumped Joseph altogether, selling him into slavery and telling their father he was dead. (You can read Joseph's story in Genesis 37-50.)

Over the years, Joseph's brothers became sorry for what they had done (they probably missed the pain in the neck). Eventually that family was reunited, and Joseph provided food and land for seventy members of his family. Joseph forgave his brothers for selling him because he was able to see the bigger picture.

> *Do not be distressed and do not be angry with yourselves for selling me here, because it was to save lives that God sent me ahead of you. . . God sent me ahead of you to preserve for you a remnant on earth and to save your lives by a great deliverance. . . You intended to harm me, but God intended it for good to accomplish what is now being done, the saving of many lives.* Genesis 45:5,7; 50:20

What's the big picture for your family? Can you imagine what your relationships will be like when all of you are grown? Write down some of your guesses about:

your relationship with your parents

_____

_____

_____

your relationship with a brother or sister

_____

_____

_____

Joseph eventually saw that God had worked in his life and family—even though it was *not* the perfect family. God knows the future, and you can trust him to work in your life and family. Pray and ask God to help you follow him in your family relationships today and to help you see God working in your lives.

☐ DAY THREE

Taking Out
the Trash

Carlos sighed as he pedalled his bike into his driveway. *Coming home isn't supposed to feel like this*, he thought, as the familiar heaviness settled on his heart.

Home Sweet Home—Ha!

Carlos's mom and dad were really struggling to keep their marriage together, and the tension between them seemed to spread through the whole house. Everyone was irritable!

Carlos found his dad in his usual place: prone on the couch in front of the TV with newspaper pages spread out all around him. Mom was on the phone in the kitchen, complaining about her husband and her overwhelming workload. His sister Lilia was hiding out in her room and didn't even answer his "hello."

Falling Short

Carlos had been a Christian for almost a year. And from his morning times in the Word of God, the teaching at his church, and the example of a few Christian families he'd encountered, he knew his family fell far short of God's ideal.

Carlos prayed for his family, and he asked God to help him live like Christ in a stressful situation. But Carlos couldn't help feeling that his efforts at encouraging, loving, and peacemaking at home were getting lost in the magnitude of the family problems.

It's like taking out two or three bags of trash when the house is full of truckloads! I can't even begin to help the problems, he thought.

Salt and Light

Ever had popcorn without salt? Pretty blah, huh? Salt is a little thing that makes a big difference. The world is like popcorn without salt—bland, without the right flavor, missing the true meaning. And Christians make up the salt of the world.

> *You are the salt of the earth. But if the salt loses its saltiness, how can it be made salty again? It is no longer good for anything, except to be thrown out and trampled by men.*
>
> *You are the light of the world. A city on a hill cannot be hidden. Neither do people light a lamp and put it under a bowl. Instead they put it on its stand, and it gives light to everyone in the house. In the same way, let your light shine before men, that they may see your good deeds and praise your Father in heaven.* Matthew 5:13-16

Carlos is living in a pretty dark situation. No wonder he feels like an itty-bitty flashlight in a pitch-black place. But his light makes a difference because it's connected to the Source of light!

How effective is your light in your home life?

_____

_____

In the "garbage" situation of your family, are you taking out the trash or piling up the heap?

_____

_____

Ask God to make you an influence for good in your family. Don't get worn out with praying for your family members who don't yet know the Lord. He's listening to your prayers!

> *The prayer of a righteous man is powerful and effective.*
> James 5:16

☐ DAY FOUR

Power
Source

Shari lay face down on her bed, crying hot tears that left a damp streak on her blue comforter. She took her journal out of the drawer in the nightstand, and looked up the entry from her birthday—less than a week earlier.

"Today I turn seventeen, and I know it's time to make some resolutions about how I treat my family. Starting today, I'm going to be patient with Harvey, and I'm not going to lose my temper and yell at Mom. I want them to know I'm a Christian for real. I know I can do it!"

Ha! she thought now, *I can't even do it for a week!* She'd been right in the middle of an important phone conversation with her best friend Paula when she realized that someone was on the other extension of the phone: Harvey. So she stomped off to throttle her little brother, and Mom came in and blamed her for the whole thing, and the next thing Shari knew she was yelling and crying.

If at First You Don't Succeed . . .

This wasn't the first time Shari had determined to live for Christ in her family. She'd tried it many times, and she just couldn't make her tongue and her temper keep her resolutions. But she kept trying. "If at first you don't succeed, try, try again" was her motto.

I've got news for Shari: it's not going to work. Sure, she needs to work hard at controlling her temper and guarding her sharp tongue. And her hard work will help—a little. But there's a much better way for Shari to tackle the temper-and-tongue project.

God's motto is different from Shari's. His says, "If at first you don't succeed, realize you need my help!"

What Could Be Better Than Jesus?

Before his death and resurrection, Jesus told his disciples, "It's good for you that I'm going away—because someone even better will come after me!" I'm sure his disciples were confused. They probably asked each other, "Who could be better than Jesus?"

> But I tell you the truth: It is for your good that I am going away. Unless I go away, the Counselor will not come to you; but if I go, I will send him to you. John 16:7

The Holy Spirit is the "Counselor" Jesus talked about. And the Holy Spirit that lives in you is your ever-ready power source for living your life for Christ.

What areas of sin do you struggle with in the way Shari struggles with keeping her temper?

_____

_____

Have you ever made resolutions to "do better"? How did it work out?

_____

_____

Have you ever asked the Lord for the Holy Spirit's power to help you in that situation?

_____

_____

Talk to God again right now about your problem areas. Thank him for the best gift, his Spirit.

> *I pray that out of his glorious riches he may strengthen you with power through his Spirit in your inner being, so that Christ may dwell in your hearts through faith. And I pray that you, being rooted and established in love, may have power, together with all the saints, to grasp how wide and long and high and deep is the love of Christ, and to know this love that surpasses knowledge—that you may be filled to the measure of all the fullness of God.* Ephesians 3:16-21

☐ DAY FIVE

The Last
Family Reunion

When was the last time you thought about heaven? Did you think about mansions, angels with harps, and streets of gold? Describe your most awesome imaginings of heaven.

_____

_____

_____

What a Neighborhood!

My family moved about a million times when I was young. (O.K.—it wasn't really that many, but sometimes it seemed like it!) And in every place we found a good church, and we made great friends. I don't write to all of those people, but I often think about them and wish we could be together again.

I don't live close to all the members of my family, either, and often I get a great big longing to see their faces instead of just talking on the phone and waiting for a vacation or for a holiday.

So it's not surprising that the picture of heaven I had when I was young was that of a giant neighborhood full of all the people I've known and loved—all living in one place close enough for me to be with them.

Face to Face

But think how it will be when we see the Lord Jesus face to face! All the frights and stresses and disappointments of the world will be gone forever, and our love for him will multiply by hundreds and hundreds in those first moments when we meet Christ's eyes.

The light of God's glory will fill the place where we, all the members of God's family, are gathered to worship. And the heavenly musicians will play fantastic music we've never heard before, music invented just for honoring God.

The Perfect Family

There, at the last great, eternal Family Reunion, we'll become the perfect family. We'll be perfectly united in worshipping God, our Maker and Creator and true Parent. We won't remember the struggles to communicate with each other and forgive one another. We'll be transformed into Christ's likeness, and we'll finally be like him!

Look forward to that day! Think of it as often as you can because remembering that you're going to live forever with God changes the way you live from day to day here on earth. Praise God now, in advance, for that great day when we will see the Lord Jesus face to face in the splendid light of his glory.

Yet to all who received him, to those who believed in his name, he gave the right to become children of God. John 1:12

And by him we cry, "Abba, Father." The Spirit himself testifies with our spirit that we are God's children. Now if we are children, then we are heirs—heirs of God and co-heirs with Christ, if indeed we share in his sufferings in order that we may also share in his glory. Romans 8:15b-17

How great is the love the Father has lavished on us, that we should be called children of God! 1 John 3:1a